Just the Facts

Global Pollution

Paul Brown

Heinemann
LIBRARY

www.heinemann.co.uk
Visit our website to find out more information about **Heinemann Library** books.

To order:
☎ Phone 44 (0) 1865 888066
🖹 Send a fax to 44 (0) 1865 314091
💻 Visit the Heinemann Bookshop at www.heinemann.co.uk to browse our catalogue and order online.

Produced by Monkey Puzzle Media Ltd, Gissing's Farm, Fressingfield, Suffolk IP21 5SH, UK

First published in Great Britain by Heinemann Library, Halley Court, Jordan Hill, Oxford OX2 8EJ, part of Harcourt Education. Heinemann is a registered trademark of Harcourt Education Ltd.

Editorial: Nick Hunter and Jennifer Tubbs
Series design: Mayer Media
Book design: Jane Hawkins
Production: Viv Hichens

Originated by Dot Gradations Ltd
Printed and bound in Hong Kong, China by South China Printers

ISBN 0 431 16146 1

06 05 04 03 02
10 9 8 7 6 5 4 3 2 1

British Library Cataloguing in Publication Data
Brown, Paul, 1944-
  Global pollution. - (Just the facts)
  1.Pollution - Juvenile literature
  I. Title
  363.7'3

Acknowledgements
The Publishers would like to thank the following for permission to reproduce photographs:
Associated Press **37** (Hermann J Knippertz); Corbis **33** (Hulton Deutsch Collection); Digital Vision **20**, **22**, **40**, **46**, **48**, **51**; Peter Bennetts **21**; Greg Evans International **45** (Greg Balfour Evans); NASA **11**; NHPA **24** (Image Quest 3-D); Novosti **17**; Popperfoto **25** (Reuters/Gordon Tomasevic); Rex Features **8** (Sipa), **9**, **29**, **34**; Science Photo Library **7**, **44** (Will and Deni McIntyre), **47** (Debra Ferguson); Still Pictures **4** (Hideo Wataka), **5** (T. Raupach), **6** (Loram Lehmann), **13** (Joerg Boething), **15** (Mark Edwards), **16** (Mark Edwards), **19** (Pascal Kobeh), **26** (Ray Pfortner), **30** (Chris James), **31** (Mike Schroder), **36** (Fritz Polking), **38** (Ron Gilling), **39** (Jeff Greenberg), **41** (Al Grillo), **43** (Mark Edwards), **49** (Angelo Doto/UNEP).

Cover photograph reproduced with permission of Environmental Images/Paul Glendell.

Every effort has been made to contact copyright holders of any material reproduced in this book. Any omissions will be rectified in subsequent printings if notice is given to the publishers.

Any words appearing in the text in bold, **like this**, are explained in the Glossary.

Contents

Introduction

Women sitting on a beach covered in litter, Japan.

Pollution comes in many forms, some more visible than others. An apparently harmless gas like carbon dioxide, which is everywhere in the air we breathe, becomes a problem if there is too much of it.

If there is too much carbon dioxide in the air – caused by burning fossil fuels like coal and oil – the temperature rises. The whole planet heats up slightly, which causes ice caps and glaciers to melt and sea levels to rise. Plants and fish species have adapted to live in certain temperatures, and if these increase they may not be able to survive: all of life on earth may eventually suffer.

Tiny amounts of an artificial substance such as **plutonium** are a danger if allowed into the environment. A single plutonium **molecule** can cause life-threatening illnesses. Such substances are described as pollutants when they begin to upset the natural balance of life on the planet, or cause people pain or injury.

On a small scale, pollution is often easily noticed and quickly tackled. Chemicals leaking into a river and killing the fish can be traced and stopped. We can smell and see smoke from a fire. The cause and the effect are easily linked and the people responsible can be found.

A global problem

Global pollution can be a more complex issue. By the time scientists have discovered there is a problem the pollution may have been going on for years, and many people in different places may be responsible. The effects are also more difficult to understand. Chemicals and plastics are made for useful purposes and make life easier, but they have unfortunate consequences when they arrive somewhere they are not wanted. An example seen almost everywhere in the world is pollution from discarded plastic bags and bottles. Even on uninhabited islands in the Pacific Ocean, thousands of miles from cities, there are often hundreds of old bags and bottles washed up at high tide. Discarded plastic and other rubbish is not just annoying and ugly, but it can trap and suffocate unwary animals, turtles, fish or birds. If properly treated, much of this material could be recycled.

The first section of this book explores the history of global pollution, and then the issues are examined in more depth in the second and third sections. The fourth section looks at what can be done to reverse the damage caused, and finally there are useful practical suggestions and facts and figures.

Chemical outflow, Germany.

The origins of pollution

Humans began to change the face of the planet many centuries ago. From earliest times, trees were cut down to make fields to grow crops, and rivers were blocked by small dams for irrigation and to make pools to grow fish for food. People have always thrown their waste away but it was not until the industrial revolution began 250 years ago that this habit was more than a local problem. Until then, most things were made of natural materials such as wood, which decayed easily when thrown away. Objects made of metal were precious, and if broken would be melted down and re-used. In the industrial revolution, new ways of mass-producing items were discovered. The power for running factories and machines meant cities were shrouded in smoke and ash, and more and more waste was produced.

In crowded cities pollution became more obvious. Rubbish had to be removed, and smoke and dirty water were a health hazard. Pouring sewage directly into the Thames in London 200 years ago was not only unpleasant, but was causing ill health. Pollution of water by **bacteria** was proved to be linked to sickness. In 1848 the first major Public Health Act was passed by parliament in the UK, which said that all towns and cities had to provide clean water. In the USA towns on rivers suffered **cholera** outbreaks and many people died. Progressive towns built sewage works to clean the water before returning it to the river, and their citizens became free of disease.

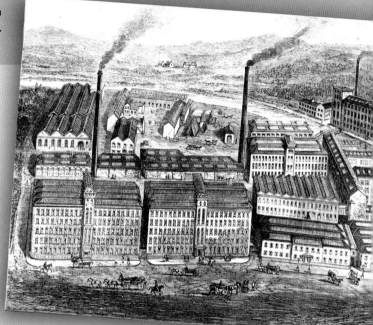

An engraving of an aerial view of textile factories in Glasgow, UK, in the 1880s.

Air pollution

Coal had been used for centuries, but when industry started to use it on a large scale from the late 18th century, smoke and fumes became a continual problem. Sulphur and soot were emitted from thousands of chimneys, causing illnesses among workers and those living near factories, as well as nuisance from dirt. Laws were passed to help prevent this; industrial chimneys had filters fitted to take out the larger particles. However, clouds of pollution persisted until the 1950s, when further laws banned the use of coal in cities.

Other great problems caused by industrial activities were not understood. When trees and crops died around industrial cities, acid fumes from factory chimneys were blamed, but to solve the problem chimneys were simply made taller, distributing the problem further away.

Over millions of years, the leaves and trunks of dead plants – buried under layers of new growth – had gradually broken down and turned into coal and oil, which are known as **fossil fuels**. When these were mined and burned as fuel, carbon dioxide – formed from the carbon in the plants – was released into the air.

In 1896, the Swedish chemist, Svante Arrhenius, published a theory forecasting that the extra carbon in the air would cause the earth to heat up. Only fellow scientists were interested in the idea.

7

Into the 20th century

Nuclear explosions

Pollution was still being treated as a local issue until 50 years ago, because it was not considered possible that an activity going on in one country could affect people in another. Nuclear bomb tests in the 1950s showed that it could. The explosions were so huge that radioactive particles were blown into the upper **atmosphere**, where powerful winds distributed them all round the world. They drifted back to earth, and people everywhere received a minute dose of radiation. Levels of radioactive material such as Strontium-90 and **plutonium** can be measured in people's teeth because this is where the material is stored when it enters the body. Even today it can still be detected. A global anti-nuclear test movement began in response to fears of cancer and genetic defects in children. In 1963 an international ban on testing in the atmosphere was signed.

The problem of fuels

Other global pollutants were not so dramatic, but were distributed by people's new uses for simple natural substances normally left in the ground. From 1921, lead was added to petrol to make engines run more smoothly. It was not known then that lead in the atmosphere could damage the human brain and nervous system. The amount of lead in the air gradually increased from 1922 onwards, but is now going down again. The reason for this improvement is that the lead-free petrol now used in the USA and Europe is being phased in around the world.

In the twentieth century, the worldwide trade in oil to power cars and industry caused pollution problems like oil tanker spills, which damaged wildlife and habitats. After the Second World War, the growth of consumer society in wealthy countries – such as Europe, the USA and Japan – dramatically increased ownership of cars, fridges and aerosol sprays. This caused the release of larger quantities of chemicals and carbon dioxide into the air. Pollution was growing fast.

Ozone

After the nuclear bomb tests, the next big atmospheric pollution issue to reach public attention was the holes in the ozone layer. The first major hole was discovered over the Antarctic in May 1985 by British scientist, Joe Farman, who was in the region studying the upper **atmosphere**. By 1996, this hole had grown to an area three times the size of the USA, and another was developing over the Arctic. Ozone is a gas in the **stratosphere** that acts like a shield. It filters out **ultraviolet** light from the sun and so protects humans, animals and plants. Scientists had predicted that artificial chemicals, **chloro-fluorocarbons** – known as **'CFCs'** – could theoretically damage the ozone layer, but no one thought it would happen on such a scale. CFCs were used as a coolant in fridges, to power aerosol sprays, and to blow foam for use in insulation and furniture. When released into the atmosphere CFCs drift upwards and react with the ozone and destroy it. As a result of this discovery, people all over the world were advised to use high-factor sun cream to protect themselves against the extra damaging rays from the sun. Children in places like Australia and New Zealand, where the ozone was thinnest, were asked to wear hats and protective clothing outdoors.

> **❝A greenhouse may be a good place to raise plants; it is no place to nurture our children.❞**
>
> (Bill Clinton, former US President, 1997)

Global warming

Scientists had already begun to worry about another danger, global warming. There has always been climate change on earth, with both ice ages and hot periods. Exactly why they happen is still not certain, although increases in carbon dioxide coincide with the hot periods. In the 1980s there was a series of hot summers and droughts. Concern was growing that these were linked with the increasing amounts of carbon dioxide and methane in the air caused by human activities. Unlike ozone these gases let the sunlight through, but when the heat rebounds off the earth they trap some of it in the same way as glass would. Scientists called this the 'greenhouse effect'.

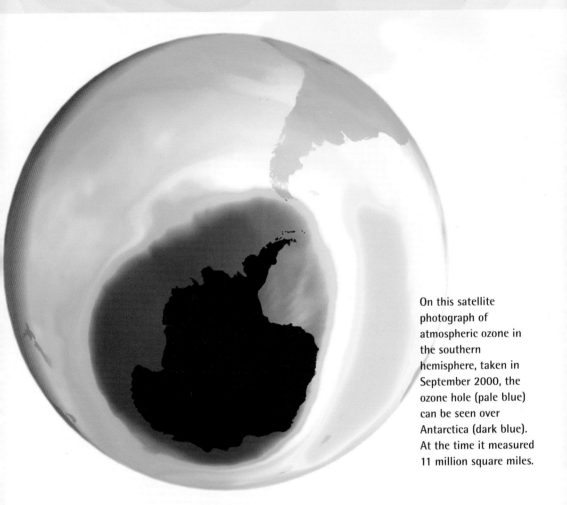

On this satellite photograph of atmospheric ozone in the southern hemisphere, taken in September 2000, the ozone hole (pale blue) can be seen over Antarctica (dark blue). At the time it measured 11 million square miles.

It was difficult to measure exactly what was happening because the weather on earth is naturally so variable. In order to be sure, scientists began careful worldwide measurements of temperature. They found **glaciers** were melting more each year, causing rivers to swell from the increased amount of water. This added to sea levels, which were already rising from the expansion of water caused by warmer temperatures. Already low-lying areas of land are regularly flooded, and many more areas will be affected or permanently lost if global warming continues.

Chemicals

Insects that eat crops or carry human diseases can be killed with insecticides, also known as pesticides. One of the first insecticides, DDT, was used extensively in the Second World War to kill mites, fleas and mosquitoes, which carried dangerous diseases like **typhus** and malaria. In this way the use of DDT saved many lives. However, a famous book, *Silent Spring* – published in 1962 by US scientist, Rachel Carson – told a different story. It revealed that DDT and other pesticides accumulate in the body fat of birds, fish and animals, including humans. *Silent Spring* shocked readers by pointing out that DDT made birds **infertile**, and so eventually there might be no more birds. This insecticide was banned in the USA in 1973 and the UK in 1984, and was replaced by less persistent alternatives. It is still in use in many parts of the world because it is a cheap and easy way of killing pests, even though it is dangerous to the people using it.

Gradually scientists realised that artificial chemicals – known as Persistent Organic Pollutants (POPs) – used to control insects and weeds could also be harmful and were spread widely round the world. These, and metals like mercury, chromium, nickel, cadmium and copper used in industry were released into the air and water and were found in food and wildlife. Tiny amounts eaten by insects in water can add up to dangerous quantities in fish that eat them. Birds, or even humans, might eventually die if they ate too many of these fish. This is an example of how pollution affects the food chain. The build up of chemicals in the body fat of seals, whales and polar bears has been found to threaten their ability to breed.

Farm workers spraying crops, India.

By 1990, with scientific evidence of global pollution threatening human health, and indeed the entire planet, mounting, there was growing public concern. Some scientists thought of a solution to the problem of pest and weed control: they could breed special crops that could resist certain types of disease or pests. They could do this by taking some of the qualities of one plant and adding it to another, by a process called genetic manipulation. For example, adding a specific **gene** taken from a snowdrop to a potato to stop slugs eating it would mean farmers could avoid using insecticides. This technology is controversial, because it is not easy to control once the new plants are in the environment. There are fears of **cross-pollination** with other crops. In the long term pests may adapt to the new plants and start damaging them again.

Who is affected by pollution?

The climate is different in every part of the earth because it is affected by the sun's heat and how close it is to the sea, but it is connected across the world by wind and weather systems. These may originate in one place and have an effect somewhere else. Wind and rain, rivers and oceans eventually distribute pollution to every country. Although it is worst at the place where it is created – at a factory belching smoke, or the end of a car exhaust – pollution is constantly diluted and spread.

Today there are 300 to 500 chemicals in the average person's body that had not been found in anyone's tissue before the 1920s. Each year thousands of new chemicals – invented by scientists to make our lives easier – are sold or used in new products. There are now more than 75,000 synthetic chemicals on the market. Often they are not fully tested to make sure they will not become pollutants. As with **CFCs** and DDT, what seems to be a very useful product may turn out to have unforeseen disadvantages. Nobody knows exactly what the long-term effects will be, but the possibilities include illness, **infertility** and birth defects.

"Increasing population and consumption are altering the planet on an unprecedented scale. Everywhere we see signs of stress – destroyed natural habitats ... polluted air and water, and melting icecaps from global warming."

(Thoraya Obaid, executive director, United Nations Population Fund, 2001)

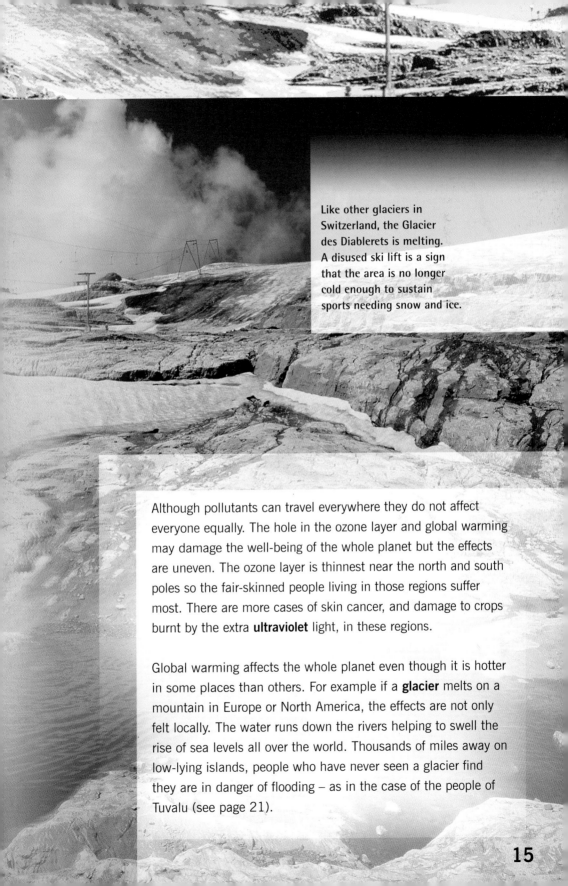

Like other glaciers in Switzerland, the Glacier des Diablerets is melting. A disused ski lift is a sign that the area is no longer cold enough to sustain sports needing snow and ice.

Although pollutants can travel everywhere they do not affect everyone equally. The hole in the ozone layer and global warming may damage the well-being of the whole planet but the effects are uneven. The ozone layer is thinnest near the north and south poles so the fair-skinned people living in those regions suffer most. There are more cases of skin cancer, and damage to crops burnt by the extra **ultraviolet** light, in these regions.

Global warming affects the whole planet even though it is hotter in some places than others. For example if a **glacier** melts on a mountain in Europe or North America, the effects are not only felt locally. The water runs down the rivers helping to swell the rise of sea levels all over the world. Thousands of miles away on low-lying islands, people who have never seen a glacier find they are in danger of flooding – as in the case of the people of Tuvalu (see page 21).

Atmospheric pollution

Acid rain

Around 50 years ago Swedish scientists realised that death of fish and damage to trees in their country was due to long-range pollution carried on the wind. Sulphur dioxide and nitrogen oxides from factory chimneys in the UK, Germany and Poland were carried thousands of miles to Scandinavia. Pollutants reacted together in the clouds, falling in rain as dilute sulphuric and nitric acid. This 'acid rain' was damaging life in lakes and rivers in many parts of the world including the USA and Asia. Populations of sensitive fish, such as salmon and trout in Scandinavia and chub and yellow perch in the USA, were plunging. Forests in Britain and Germany had begun to die. An international effort began, to reduce the level of sulphur emissions – the primary cause. The problem is still enormous. In Sweden 20,000 of the 90,000 lakes in the country are damaged by acid rain. In order to maintain life in 8000 of the worst affected, lime – which is alkaline – is added to the water to counteract the acid. Huge areas of forest soil are sprinkled with lime to help recovery. The only long-term solution is to reduce emissions further. In order to do this, countries must agree to limit and control industrial and other activities where coal and oil are burned.

Spraying a polluted Swedish lake with lime, to counteract acid.

An aerial view of the remains of the Chernobyl nuclear power station during the early stages of making the reactor safe.

Nuclear accidents

The role of rain in washing pollution out of the sky became more widely understood after the Chernobyl nuclear power station accident in Russia in 1986. The accident happened when a nuclear reactor suffered an explosion, discharging vast amounts of radioactivity into the sky over several days. **Fallout** from this accident affected many countries in Europe, depending on which way the wind blew and where rain fell. In Britain it rained a week after the accident, pouring radioactive material from Chernobyl on to the grass in North Wales and Cumbria. Some sheep from these areas still cannot be sold for food sixteen years later because they contain too much radioactivity. Around Chernobyl itself the situation is far worse, with many children in the fallout area developing cancer.

Climate change

The greatest long-term threat to the planet is climate change. In 1988 the United Nations put together the grandly named Intergovernmental Panel on Climate Change to investigate. With 1500 of the best brains from every country in the world, it was the largest number of scientists ever gathered together on one issue. The biggest computers in the world were used to forecast what would happen. These forecasts were compared with measurements of what was actually happening. The idea was to find out how the world's climate was already changing and to predict future trends. These reports are still being produced.

At first the scientists were uncertain, but they became more convinced that human pollution was interfering with the climate and causing the 'greenhouse effect'. Already, because the climate was warmer, birds were nesting two weeks earlier in Europe and North America. Snow was not falling as far south in winter as it once did, and was melting sooner. Crops had longer to grow, and leaves came out earlier in spring.

Extra heat in Africa means some places can no longer grow crops at all. In the USA and Russia it will be possible to grow grain further north, but the US Great Plains are drying out. Forests in the north-eastern Amazon in South America are beginning to die. In Alaska, Russia and China buildings, roads and railways built on the assumption that the frozen ground would remain solid as rock, have collapsed as the **permafrost** has begun to melt. Coral reefs have been killed by excessive sea temperatures destroying breeding grounds for fish. Flooding, already an increasing problem in many areas including Western Europe, is set to get worse. Natural disasters like hurricanes are on the increase, and food and water supplies are threatened. The future still remains uncertain, because it is difficult to predict exactly how the climate will change and what effects this will have. Will forests be able to adapt to higher temperatures? To prevent disasters scientists recommend a cut of 60 per cent in the world's carbon emissions to stabilize the climate. This can be achieved by limiting the use of **fossil fuels**. For example, vehicle use can be controlled by measures such as taxing drivers of larger vehicles, or those who drive in cities. Public transport can be improved and promoted to reduce the number of cars on the roads. New types of fuel and sources of power are being developed.

Bleached and dying coral. Coral is the first eco-system to suffer critically from global warming and acts as an indicator of serious damage.

Rising sea levels

Around the world, sea levels are already rising. Stormy weather is causing bigger waves in the Atlantic Ocean and tides are reaching record levels. On average sea levels rose by 20 to 30 centimetres (8–12 inches) in the last century, and the process is accelerating. The rise is expected to be three times that much in the next 100 years. This is partly because water in the oceans expands as it gets warmer. Many scientists believe that ice-caps and glaciers are melting on a greater scale than before and adding to the volume of water in rivers and seas. The increase may not sound like very much, but many of the world's biggest food growing areas are on the coast. Bangladesh, Egypt, Vietnam and China grow most of their food less than 1 metre above sea level. Large parts of Florida would be flooded without big, expensive sea walls. London and New York are among many cities in danger because of this sea level rise.

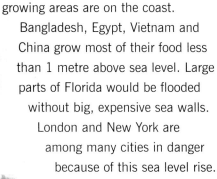

Tuvalu

Tuvalu, mid-way between Hawaii and Australia in the Pacific Ocean, is a small island state where 11,000 people live on nine coral islands. None of the islands is more than 2 metres above sea level. They look very beautiful with sandy beaches and palm trees, but they have no hills and are vulnerable to rising sea levels. Parts of the islands have already flooded. Salt water has entered the wells making it difficult to find fresh water to drink. It is becoming almost impossible to grow crops because of salt intrusion. Coastal erosion is eating away at the islands and so the islanders have decided to abandon their homeland. New Zealand has agreed to take all of them, under an evacuation plan starting in 2002. Tuvalu seems likely to be the first country to disappear because of climate change, but there will be others. South of India is the popular holiday country of the Maldives, also built on coral islands. This time there are 1196 tiny islands supporting 311,000 people. These islands could all be overtopped by a sea level rise of 1 metre. Where will the people go?

❝We are an endangered nation.❞

(Abdul Gayoom, president of the Maldives, in a speech to the UN, 2000)

Water pollution

Lack of clean water is becoming a critical problem in large parts of the world. The situation is rapidly getting worse and most affects the poorest people. In rich countries, clean water coming out of the tap fit to drink, wash or cook is taken for granted. For 1.1 billion (1.1 thousand million) people in poor countries clean water is unobtainable, even from taps in the street, or wells. As a result 15 million children under five die each year because of diseases caused by drinking unclean water.

One of the major problems is lack of sanitation. Sewage is flushed straight back into streams and rivers without being cleaned. Fresh water, which could be used, is wasted, and disease is spread. Almost half the world's population, especially in rural areas, does not have proper drains and waste disposal.

Growing population, climate change, and increasing use of water for **irrigation** and industry are making the situation worse. So much water is taken out of some rivers that they are reduced to a trickle. The Yellow River in China, one of the longest in the world, had so much water taken for irrigation each summer that it ran dry 600 kilometres (400 miles) upstream from the river's mouth every year during the 1990s. The Rio Grande River on the US-Mexico border developed a sandbar across its mouth showing there was almost no flow into the sea.

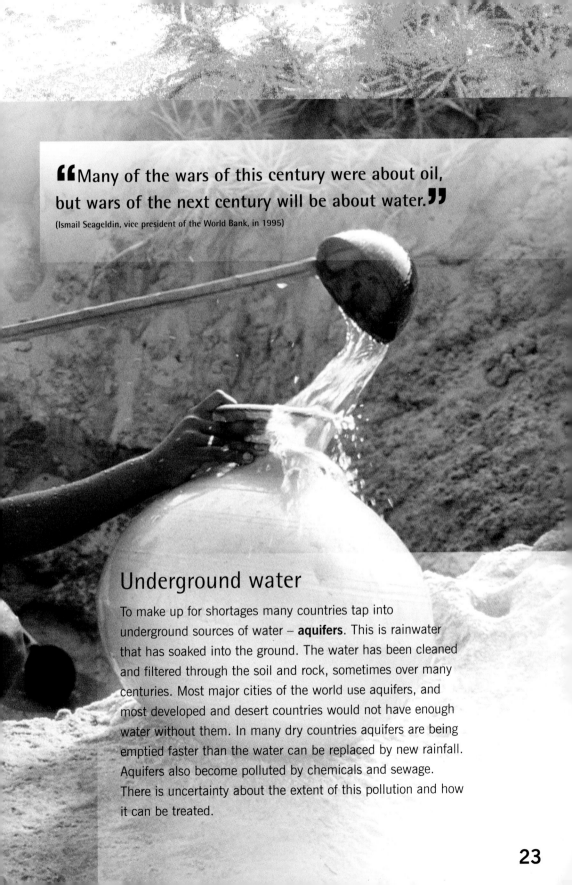

Underground water

To make up for shortages many countries tap into underground sources of water – **aquifers**. This is rainwater that has soaked into the ground. The water has been cleaned and filtered through the soil and rock, sometimes over many centuries. Most major cities of the world use aquifers, and most developed and desert countries would not have enough water without them. In many dry countries aquifers are being emptied faster than the water can be replaced by new rainfall. Aquifers also become polluted by chemicals and sewage. There is uncertainty about the extent of this pollution and how it can be treated.

The Black Sea

The Black Sea was once so productive that whole civilizations flourished on its banks and its fish harvest was exported across Europe. Now it is so heavily polluted, the monk seals have disappeared, and many of the 47 fish species have become extinct.

Six countries have coastlines on the Black Sea, all of which pour sewage and industrial rubbish into its waters. Many long rivers – including Europe's biggest, the Danube – empty into the Black Sea, bringing with them more waste from countries that are hundreds of miles away. Altogether 21 nations and 160 million people contribute towards pollution around the Black Sea.

The main problem is sewage, which contains nitrogen and phosphorus. There are many inefficient sewage works and some that do not work at all. Agricultural fertilizers washed from fields into rivers and then into the sea add more of the same chemicals. **Algae** feed on these chemicals, and multiply into huge carpets on the surface of the water, blocking out the light. Plants under the surface, deprived of light, can no longer produce oxygen, and the fish eventually suffocate. At Odessa, once a Black Sea holiday resort, bathing is banned after outbreaks of **cholera** and **dysentery** caused by the polluted water.

Jellyfish, along with chemical pollution, helped destroy other life forms in the Black Sea.

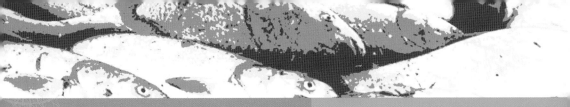

A workman removes dead fish after a cyanide spill in Romania reached the River Danube, which flows into the Black Sea.

Another problem is jellyfish, properly known as comb jellies. In 1987, some trading ships from the Great Lakes of North America accidentally carried tiny jellyfish in water that had seeped into the bottom of the ships. This water, known as bilge-water, is pumped out at the end of a trip. On this occasion the water was pumped out with the young jellyfish. Comb jellies eat the young of local fish and they liked the Black Sea so much that numbers grew to billions. By 1997, sailors joked that they did not sail across the sea, they slithered on the 700 million tonnes of jellyfish. The fishing became so poor that fleets of boats were tied up and left rusting in harbour.

The countries in the region realize what a terrible mistake this pollution has been, and they are trying to save the sea. One project is to restore the giant reed beds at the mouth of the River Danube. Reeds literally eat the excess nutrients that cause algae blooms that pollute the river. They help clean the water before it reaches the sea. This is already working, although much more needs to be done.

Land pollution

The average family in Europe and Australia throws away a tonne of rubbish a year. In North America it is sometimes double that, and the volume is growing all the time. All over the world household waste is an increasing problem. Tins and plastic containers are used once and thrown away. Governments are making efforts to reduce this by passing laws to minimize packaging, and encouraging reuse and recycling. However, most of this rubbish still gets dumped in holes in the ground, which are often left by quarrying. Some rubbish is burned to reduce the volume, but this leaves large quantities of ash. Burning or incinerating rubbish also produces harmful **toxins**, which add to air pollution.

Industry produces vast amounts of waste, some of it **toxic**. In some countries it is tipped on the land but in richer countries, with stricter laws, it has to be taken to special works and treated before it can be dumped.

Despite these precautions there are large areas in all countries where land is contaminated. This is particularly found in old industrial areas, which can be full of unknown chemicals, heavy metals – like lead and mercury, which can cause brain damage – and poisons like arsenic. Sometimes there are slag heaps – ash, coal or metal waste – from old iron works or mine workings. Often the soil is so damaged that very little will grow and it is dangerous to graze animals or build houses there.

The problem of landfill of industrial and household rubbish is made worse because the rubbish mixes with rainwater and rots, producing gas.

This is often methane, which is a 'greenhouse' gas, adding to the problem of global warming. Contaminated water can also run into streams and drinking water causing danger to wildlife and humans.

Land can also be contaminated on a large scale by bad irrigation practices. In very dry countries large areas are soaked in water from rivers to grow crops. Because the weather is hot the water evaporates quickly leaving behind tiny quantities of salt. Unless there is regular clean rainfall to wash the soil this salt builds up, contaminating the land. Often it becomes so salty that normal crops will no longer grow.

Household waste is dumped in a landfill site.

Environment versus development

Governments in poorer countries fear that demands from the richer industrial world that they must preserve their environment will prevent economic development. If everyone in the USA has a car, a television and a fridge why is it wrong for people in China and India to want the same?

However, the opposite argument can also be put. If there is too much carbon dioxide being produced already what will happen to the climate when the 2 billion (2 million million) people currently with no electricity get to switch electric lights on?

These were key questions in 1992 when the nations of the world met in the Brazilian city of Rio de Janeiro for what was called the Conference on Environment and Development, but has become known as the Earth Summit. They caused many divisions between rich and poor countries. Some of the rich countries were concerned about global warming, loss of forests, and **biodiversity**. Some of the poor countries wanted more development, and aid from the rich countries to help them achieve it. Others pointed out that the rich industrialized nations caused the pollution in the first place.

A typical argument involved Malaysia, a developing industrial country, which came under great pressure to stop chopping down its forests. Representatives from the rich countries feared the release of the carbon in the trees would add to global warming. When trees are cut down the large quantities of carbon stored in the trunks and branches are

"Economic growth ... is essential to improve the livelihoods of the poor, to sustain growing populations, and eventually to stabilize population levels. New technologies will be needed to permit growth while using resources more efficiently and producing less pollution."

(Stephen Schmidheiny, founder, World Business Council on Sustainable Development)

released back into the atmosphere as carbon dioxide. If the forests are not replanted then there are fewer trees on the earth to absorb surplus carbon dioxide. These people were also worried that birds and animals would lose their **habitats** and might become extinct. The Malaysian government replied that the country needed the money from log sales to fund industrial development. It also reminded countries like the UK that they had cut many of their own trees down 1000 years ago to grow crops.

Despite this there were agreements that the environment must be protected. While at the same time it was acknowledged that poorer countries should have the right to develop.

Old industries fight for survival

Old industries like coal mining, coal-fired power stations and steel and chemical plants, contribute greatly to pollution, but they also employ many people. The owners and managers within such industries fear the pressure to clean up the environment, because buying or converting to new technologies will be expensive in the short term, with the possibility of job losses.

In the electricity generating business, burning coal rather than gas produces 30 per cent more carbon dioxide to provide the same amount of power. In the UK in the 1990s many coal-fired power stations were closed down and replaced with more efficient gas plants. The result was an instant saving of carbon dioxide – about 10 per cent of all UK emissions. It also reduced acid rain because there is no sulphur in gas. But many miners and power station workers were thrown out of work as a result. Fewer new jobs were created in the gas plants. The coal industries in the USA and Australia, fearing the same fate as

European businesses, have been fighting hard against global warming measures in their own countries as a result.

However, government regulations aimed at making the air cleaner are ensuring that companies adopt new technologies or face the expense of fitting filters to power stations. They may also have to pay taxes for causing pollution. If the pressure to cut down emissions of global warming gases continues, whole sectors of the economy will have to change, and some will shut down.

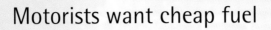

Motorists want cheap fuel

It is difficult for individuals to accept changes, even though they may want a clean environment. Motorists in the USA can buy fuel at a quarter of the UK price. As a result, even though most US cars are bigger than European ones and use more fuel, it is cheaper to drive in the USA. Politicians there have been reluctant to change this situation. Increasing fuel taxes would encourage smaller cars, cut some car use and so reduce the amount of pollution. However, it would still be unpopular with many voters, partly because people enjoy driving, and partly because public transport is poor in some countries. Oil companies are also against increasing taxes because it would damage their profits.

Similarly, air travel accounts for an increasingly large percentage of the world's carbon dioxide emission, yet there is currently no tax on aviation fuel. This is because governments wish to support the aviation industry, seeing air travel and airport development as good for business investment and the economy.

Motorway traffic jam, Berlin, Germany.

Nuclear power

The world's first nuclear power station opened in Cumbria in the UK, in 1956. Within 20 years hundreds were being built across the world. At the time it was said atomic energy would be so cheap it could replace coal and oil as the world's major energy source.

Some were not so sure, believing it was a potentially dangerous technology – because of the risk of accidents causing the release of radioactive material into the environment. Both the USA and the UK were keen on nuclear power, although some countries, like New Zealand, were opposed to the technology and did not adopt it.

The USA stopped building new nuclear power stations in the 1980s and most other countries followed in the 1990s. This was partly because of an accident at the Three Mile Island nuclear reactor in the USA in 1979, and the Chernobyl disaster of 1986 when an explosion caused radioactivity over a huge area. Hundreds of people died and thousands of children have become sick as a result. Another reason for moving away from nuclear power was because atomic energy did not turn out to be cheap after all. All the safety features that have to be built into nuclear power stations mean that power is more expensive to produce than coal, gas or **renewable energy**, such as wind power.

Despite this there is renewed interest in the technology because it produces electricity without creating greenhouse gases. Currently nuclear power produces 17 per cent of the world's electricity, and just over 20 per cent in the UK and the USA. In France, 77 per cent of all power comes from nuclear sources.

One form of pollution or another?

Many people support building new nuclear power stations to replace the older ones which are now closing down. Without them they say the production of greenhouse gases will get far worse. Others argue that turning back to nuclear power replaces one form of pollution with another. The radioactive waste that nuclear power stations produce has to be disposed of safely. Neither the UK nor the USA has come up with a solution for where to put it, except for proposing to store it in strong bunkers or underground. Radioactivity remains dangerous for 250,000 years, so future generations must be protected from any leakage.

Those opposed to the construction of new nuclear power stations believe the money would be better invested in energy conservation measures, and in new technologies such as wind, wave and solar power.

Calder Hall, the world's first nuclear power station, photographed in 1956.

Uncertain science

It is impossible to foretell the future, so the effects of pollution on the planet are very difficult to predict. The hole in the ozone layer came as a surprise to many people. The radioactivity that was distributed round the planet after nuclear tests in the 1950s had not been expected.

In the 1970s a few leading scientists believed that the world was entering a new ice age, because the weather had been colder for a few years. Others who were studying the climate came to the opposite view ten years later. When they began to say global warming was on the way it took time before they were taken seriously. Now the vast majority of scientific bodies around the world agree that it is a reality.

Detailed study of the problem by 1500 scientists, aided by the world's best computers, has still left questions unanswered. Predictions of how much the world will heat up in the next century vary

"To many environmentalists, climate change seems to be nature's revenge on humanity for economic growth."

(Frances Cairncross, writing in *The Economist* magazine)

between 1.4°C (Celsius) and 5.8°C. Scientists are very cautious but point out that anything as high as 3.5°C would be disastrous. This would mean the continuation of problems like melting ice, rising sea levels, destruction of **habitats** and dying plants and animals.

The situation has been made worse by pollutants having different effects. For example, smoke and sulphur from power stations have one good effect in that they reflect the sun's heat back to space. Curing one pollutant, acid rain, therefore might actually make the earth heat up more. Extra clouds caused by greater evaporation from the warmer

oceans add to global warming in one way and reduce it in another. Clouds act like a blanket to keep the earth warm at night but during the day reflect the sunlight back.

For these reasons there is continued uncertainty about what is going to happen. For some people this is not an excuse to do nothing: the risk of a catastrophe because of rapid climate change is too great. In any event, they say, getting rid of pollution would be a goal in itself.

Others believe the uncertainties are so great it is too early to take action. For many the loss of jobs in the coal, automobile and oil industries is too high a price to pay to solve a problem that might not become a serious threat in their own lifetimes.

Industrial pollution is a common sight throughout the developed world. Investing in clean and efficient new technology will reduce the threat of climate change.

Pressure groups

Campaigning organizations trying to influence governments have always existed. Most great social reforms – like the abolition of slavery, or women's right to vote – have begun with pressure from groups. The 1980s saw a great period of expansion for environmental campaigning groups as people across the world became aware of issues like global pollution. Membership was measured in millions and they become international organizations, with branches in dozens of countries.

There are thousands of groups, each seeing itself with a different role, some far more radical than others. In the USA and Europe there are organizations like Earth First. This is a group whose actions sometimes border on the criminal, for example putting spikes in trees (without harming the trees) to break the chain saws of loggers cutting forests down. At the other extreme are groups like the San Francisco based Sierra Club. This is supported by professional people, who offer practical help to, and **endorse**, politicians who try to protect the environment. They also produce reports, investigate and criticize those leaders whom they believe are doing the opposite.

Among the highest profile international organizations are Greenpeace and Friends of the Earth and WWF: the global environment network. They campaign on a wide variety of issues, against forest destruction, in favour of renewable energies like wind and solar, or trying to stop activities that lead to chemical pollution. All employ scientists to investigate pollution problems, and **lobbyists** and press officers, whose job it is to contact political leaders and journalists.

Expanding roles

Over time the role of such organizations changes. WWF and other groups used to campaign for particular wild animals – such as the panda or the elephant – to be protected. However they have realized that if pollution threatens to kill the animals and birds or destroy their **habitats**, then these threats need to be confronted too. They now campaign in a wider way, with other pressure groups, to curb pollution.

Young Greenpeace activists protest in Bonn, Germany, during the UN Convention on Climate Change, 2001.

Both sides have a view

Pressure on politicians and information fed to journalists is not all from pressure groups, as much comes from industry and others with particular interests. Those involved in industry have strong views and campaign to keep their businesses alive. Trade unions have a duty to protect their members and help them to keep their jobs.

Industries often form pressure groups to push their point of view. For example, the chemical industries have their own associations, which point out that excessive restrictions on chemical use might damage their member companies.

At international treaty negotiations where limits may be placed on pollution, or protection granted to endangered species, pressure groups from both sides of the argument are represented. Governments recognize these groups are important and have the right to put forward the views of the people they represent.

Sometimes the names can be confusing. The Climate Action Network, for example, represents those who would try and reduce emissions of carbon dioxide and other greenhouse gas emissions. The Climate Change Coalition was a group of coal, oil and automobile interests protecting their industries. It has now been disbanded.

Objective information

Some organizations, like the Worldwatch
Institute based in Washington D.C., are
particularly good at writing reports on
issues like water shortages, food
production, or pollution. These are
designed to increase public knowledge
of the crisis facing the planet.

In a recent report Worldwatch said that US
drivers use 43 per cent of the world's
gasoline (petrol) to propel less than 5 per
cent of the world's population around in
their cars. In China most people ride on
bicycles, but would like to drive cars. There
are more than four times as many Chinese
as Americans. If the Chinese reached the
same level of car use as people in San
Francisco did in 1990, the amount of
carbon emissions in urban China alone
would be roughly the same as released
from all the cars in the world in 1998.
It would also mean that the cities of China
would be so clogged with cars nothing
could move. This is a strictly mathematical
exercise to show the serious difficulties
facing crowded cities if the pattern of US
development and transport is followed
elsewhere. Worldwatch leaves the reader to
decide whether increased car use would be
good for the planet.

Cleaning up

The obvious solution to pollution is to clean it up. This is easier said than done: spill a drink on the carpet and it leaves a stain. So it is with oil and chemical spills. They often leave a long-term mark on the environment that is difficult to erase.

Fortunately, the natural world has many ways of adjusting to pollution. In the Gulf War of 1991, invading Iraqi troops turned on giant taps at an oil terminal in Kuwait to create the biggest oil spills of all time. This was to prevent attack from warships approaching Kuwait. Many people thought that the fish and other wildlife in the sea would die and the area would be polluted for years. In fact, the Persian Gulf had a wonderful self-cleaning mechanism. As one of the biggest oil producing areas in the world there are constant small spills of oil. In the sea are naturally occurring **microbes** that eat oil. Because of the history of the area there was a large population of these tiny animals waiting for the next spill. They multiplied and literally ate the largest oil spill on earth.

Sadly it is not always that easy. When a ship called the *Exxon Valdez* spilled 11 million gallons of oil in Alaska in 1989 there were no helpful microbes – it was too cold for them to survive. Despite the best efforts of teams of hundreds of people to disperse the oil with detergents and to pick it up with shovels the oil remained for years. Local bird and animal populations have still not fully recovered.

Other pollutants can be neutralized (for example, the effects of acid rain can be neutralized with lime) and eventually all chemicals break down in the environment, but it can take hundreds of years.

Cleaning polluted beaches after the *Exxon Valdez* oil spill in Alaska.

Fixing climate change

There have been lots of suggestions for reducing global warming, including ideas like floating giant mirrors in space to reflect back the sunlight. Adding nutrients to the sea to help carbon dioxide-eating plants to grow is being tried. When the plants die and sink they take the carbon in their bodies, storing it in the mud. Norway has successfully pioneered pumping carbon dioxide down into old oil and gas wells under the sea to stop it reaching the atmosphere, but this is expensive. Environmentalists believe it would be easier to avoid pollution in the first place.

International treaties

Countries often try to co-operate by making treaties and alliances. Since the mid-20th century, concerns that pollution from one country was reaching another have led to a new era of international co-operation on the environment. The problem of acid rain led to the first European agreements to limit sulphur emissions, in 1982. Countries realized that clean water and healthy trees and animals would benefit everyone. These agreements were strengthened in 1994.

The most comprehensive international agreement that changed the way global pollution was tackled was the **Montreal Protocol** of 1987. This agreement covered the whole world, and all the countries that produced **CFCs** accepted that to save the ozone layer these chemicals had to be replaced with safer ones.

Every year the main countries in the Protocol meet to review progress. Because the chemicals that attack the ozone layer live so long in the atmosphere, the ozone hole is still getting bigger. When these chemicals disappear, the natural processes that provide a protective layer of ozone will work unhindered once again, and it is hoped that by 2050 ozone should return to normal levels.

Earth Summit

At the Earth Summit of 1992, in Rio de Janeiro, treaties to deal with other global threats were negotiated. They included the Climate Change Convention, to tackle global warming, and the **Biodiversity** Convention to protect natural **habitats**. Later, a Desertification Convention was signed to prevent the further spread of deserts, although a hoped-for treaty to conserve forests has never been completed.

In 1997 the **Kyoto Protocol** was added to the Climate Change Convention. This gave every industrial country a target to control and reduce its greenhouse gas emissions. The details proved very difficult to negotiate. In 2001 the USA pulled out of its own agreement to reduce emissions by 7 per cent by 2012. Many Americans, including the President, George W. Bush, felt the agreement was unfair. They said the cost of cutting the US emissions would be more for them than for other countries, because more **fossil fuel** is used per head in the USA than in any other country.

The rest of the world decided to continue without the USA, but hopes it will rejoin the agreement. The USA is vitally important because on its own the country produces 25 per cent of all the world's carbon dioxide emissions. Most people accept that unless these emissions are cut there is little hope of limiting global warming.

Tree of Life sculpture at the Earth Summit in 1992.

Finding alternatives

Renewables

Most people accept that **renewable energy** is the way forward. This is not just because pollution from burning **fossil fuels** is damaging the environment and we ought to find cleaner ways of making electricity and running our cars; it is also because supplies of coal, oil and gas will eventually run out, while renewable energy will not.

There are many new technologies on offer, some of which are already well established and support large industries. Wind power is the best example. As the design of wind **turbines** has improved the cost of generating electricity by this method has reduced, and in many places it is cheaper than using fossil fuels. **Geothermal power** is another method of generating energy, where cold water is piped through naturally hot rocks to create steam to drive generators. This can only work in areas where there are hot rocks near the surface of the earth.

Wave and solar power are now rapidly being developed to provide electricity. Harnessing the power of waves is technically difficult but has great promise in countries like the UK and Australia, with long coastlines. The power of solar energy has great potential. It is, after all, the heat from the sun that supports life on earth and drives the weather and ocean currents.

Many scientists believe **hydrogen** is the fuel of the future. It produces no pollutants when it burns and there are unlimited supplies. The problem is isolating and containing it in a form that can be used to power cars and to make electricity. If solar power could be used to produce large quantities of cheap hydrogen many of the world's power and pollution problems could be solved. Companies are spending huge sums on research and development in this area.

Recycling

People often throw things away instead of reusing or recycling them. Recycling can save a lot of energy and natural resources by reusing materials that would otherwise be thrown away. Far more energy is used in making a new aluminium can than in melting down an old one and reusing the material. The more energy is used, the more power is needed to produce it.

Recycling also reduces the amount of waste going to landfill. This saves valuable space and cuts down on pollution.

❝A combination of wind turbines, solar cells, hydrogen generators, and fuel cell engines offers not only energy independence, but an alternative to climate-disrupting fossil fuels.❞

(Lester R. Brown, president of the Earth Policy Institute, Washington D.C.)

Drinks cans compacted into blocks prior to recycling.

What can you do?

Save energy

This is important because the less energy we use, the less power is needed to produce it. That means fewer emissions and less carbon dioxide (the main global warming gas) in the air. Here are some of things you, your family and school can do:

Turn down the thermostat on your heating by 1°C.

In the UK alone £200 million a year is spent leaving televisions, computers and other machines on standby. Save energy by switching off.

Use low-energy light bulbs: they run five times as long on one fifth of the electricity.

When you boil a kettle, use only the amount of water you need. If everyone in the UK did this for just one day it would save enough electricity to keep every street lamp in the country on, the following night.

Choose local products, especially food. Apples and other fruit are often flown round the world while local farmers cannot sell their own, thus adding to air pollution.

Old refrigerators contain CFCs and should be disposed of carefully.

Avoid chemicals

Most batteries contain toxic chemicals that leak into the environment when thrown away. Buy re-chargeable, solar or non-toxic ones.

Do not throw mobile phones or computers away; take them for recycling, reuse or safe disposal. They contain toxic chemicals.

Cotton is the world's most heavily sprayed crop. Pesticide run-off poisons rivers, water supplies and wildlife. Look for **organic** cotton and wool.

Buy organic food, which has been produced without the use of artificial chemicals.

Save energy and cut down on landfill

Buy recycled products whenever you can. By buying them you create a market and encourage more recycling. Consolidate all your shopping in one bag rather than get a new one at each shop. Even better, take your own shopping bag with you. Waste caused by plastic bags is a major problem all around the world.

Buy recycled paper. Do not discard paper until you have used both sides. When you have finished with it, take it to a paper collection bank.

Recycling just one plastic bottle can save the energy needed to power a 60 watt light bulb for six hours. Huge numbers of plastic bottles are thrown away every day.

Recycle glass, plastic, paper and cans, sorting the items carefully.

Start a compost heap and recycle scraps of uncooked food. You can buy a compost bin ready made or you can build your own. Worms will be attracted naturally but it is possible to acquire tiger worms or red worms. They breed quickly in warm compost and eat up to half their bodyweight each day, producing rich, dark compost for the garden. If you do not have a garden there may be a local composting project. If everyone composted it would save one third of all the waste currently dumped in landfill.

"Solutions start at home, with you and me."

(Charles Secrett, Director, Friends of the Earth UK)